Big Shark's Lost Tooth

To Julia and Nancy
—S.M.

To my parents
—M.B.

ISBN 0-439-83746-4

12 11 10 9 8 7 6 5 4 3 2 6 7 8 9 10 11/0

Book design by Jennifer Rinaldi Windau

Printed in the U.S.A.

First printing, January 2006

Big Shark's Lost Tooth

by Steve Metzger

Illustrated by Michelle Barbera

SCHOLASTIC INC.

New York Toronto London Auckland Sydney
Mexico City New Delhi Hong Kong Buenos Aires

Chomp was a big lemon shark who loved playing hide-and-seek with his best friends, Ollie the Octopus and Minnie the Manta Ray.

"Minnie will never find me here!" Chomp said as he ducked behind a rock. He happily took a bite out of his Coral-reef Crunch bar.

He felt something hard that wouldn't crunch.

It was his tooth! It had fallen out!

"Wow!" Chomp said.

"I found you!" Minnie said. "You were making too much noise."

"I don't care," said Chomp. "Look at this!"

"It's too bad the Tooth Fairy doesn't visit the ocean," Minnie said.

"Why not?" Chomp asked.

"I don't know," Minnie replied. "She just visits boys and girls who live on land."

"No fair!" Chomp said as he swam toward home.

Chomp found his mother working in her garden.

"It's not fair!" Chomp shouted.

"What's not fair, sweetie?" she asked.

"The Tooth Fairy!" Chomp said. "I lost my first tooth, and the Tooth Fairy won't visit me!"

Chomp showed his mother the tooth.

"It's a beauty!" she said. "Maybe the Tooth Fairy will come. You never know."

That night, Chomp put the tooth under his seaweed pillow.

"I really hope she visits me," Chomp said. "Just like she visits the boys and girls on land."

"Me, too," Chomp's mother said. "And there's going to be lots more lost teeth. Young lemon sharks like you lose an entire set of teeth every week."

"Is that really true?" Chomp asked.

"Absolutely!" she replied. "But as you lose teeth, new ones will quickly replace them."

After he fell asleep, Chomp's mother searched the ocean floor for a gift.

I don't want Chomp to be disappointed, she thought. *But I've never heard of the Tooth Fairy coming to the bottom of the ocean.* Finally, she found a sand dollar near a sea anemone.

"I hope he likes this," she said as she replaced Chomp's tooth with the sand dollar. But when his mother accidentally bumped into him, Chomp woke up.

"You're not the Tooth Fairy!" Chomp shouted.

He angrily jumped out of bed and looked for something to bite. He found an old piece of wood and bit into it. Another tooth fell out, and Chomp began to cry.

"I'm sorry you're so sad," Chomp's mother said. "I'm going to do whatever I can to get the Tooth Fairy to come here for this tooth."

Chomp fell asleep and dreamed that the Tooth Fairy visited him.

The next day while Chomp was busy playing, his mother secretly wrote a letter to the Tooth Fairy.

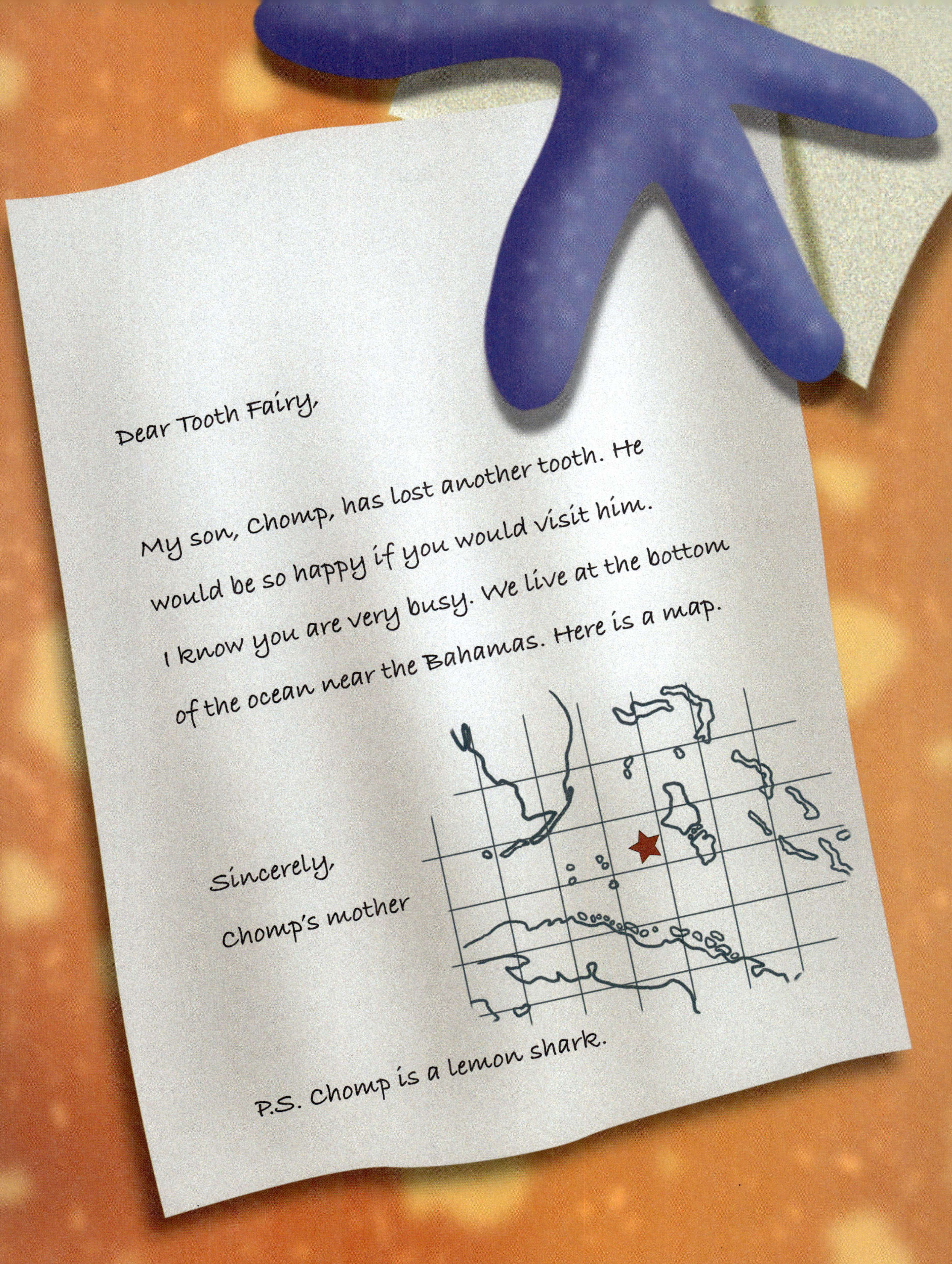
Dear Tooth Fairy,

My son, Chomp, has lost another tooth. He would be so happy if you would visit him. I know you are very busy. We live at the bottom of the ocean near the Bahamas. Here is a map.

Sincerely,
Chomp's mother

P.S. Chomp is a lemon shark.

Now, how can I get this message to the Tooth Fairy? Chomp's mother wondered.

"I know!" she exclaimed. "Gertie the Seagull! She knows everyone, and she's always willing to help an old friend." She began to swim away.

"What's going on, Mom?" Chomp asked.

"I have an errand to run," she replied. "I'll be right back."

Chomp's mother swam as fast as she could to the ocean's surface. The other sea creatures quickly darted out of her way.

"Gertie! Gertie!" she called out. After a few minutes, Gertie the Seagull flew overhead.

"Mabel, you sharp-toothed rascal, what brings you up here?" Gertie asked.

"Can you please deliver this note to the Tooth Fairy? It's very important."

"Sure," Gertie replied. "Anything for you." And off she went. Gertie flew to the top of Fairy Mountain and into the Tooth Fairy's castle.

After a busy night of visiting boys and girls all over the world, the Tooth Fairy was still fast asleep.

Gertie dropped the note from Chomp's mother next to the Tooth Fairy's pillow and started to fly away.

The Tooth Fairy awoke with a start. "What are you doing here?" she called out. "Come back!" But Gertie was gone.

The Tooth Fairy noticed the letter and read it. When she finished, she shouted, "A LEMON SHARK! How *exciting*!"

Floss

The Tooth Fairy grabbed her magic bag and flew out the window. She flew for hours and hours, checking her map along the way. As the sun went down, the Tooth Fairy arrived at the right spot. She dove into the water.

Racing past colorful jellyfish, playful sea horses, and a scary swordfish, she found Chomp's mother watching him as he slept. Chomp had already put his tooth under the pillow.

"Maybe the Tooth Fairy will come tonight," Chomp's mother said in a soft voice. Then she turned and saw that the Tooth Fairy was standing right next to her!

"Is it really you?" Chomp's mother whispered.

"Yes, indeed," the Tooth Fairy replied. "I just *had* to come after reading your letter." The Tooth Fairy reached into her bag and replaced Chomp's tooth with her gift.

"Now I must go," she said. "There are so many children I still need to visit."

"Good-bye, Tooth Fairy," Chomp's mother said. "Thank you so much for coming."

In an instant, the Tooth Fairy was gone.

The next morning, Chomp woke up and immediately looked under his pillow. "It's a sparkly crystal!" he said. It was the most wonderful thing he had *ever* seen. "Was the Tooth Fairy really here?" Chomp asked.

Chomp's mother nodded. "Look! She wrote something on the bottom."

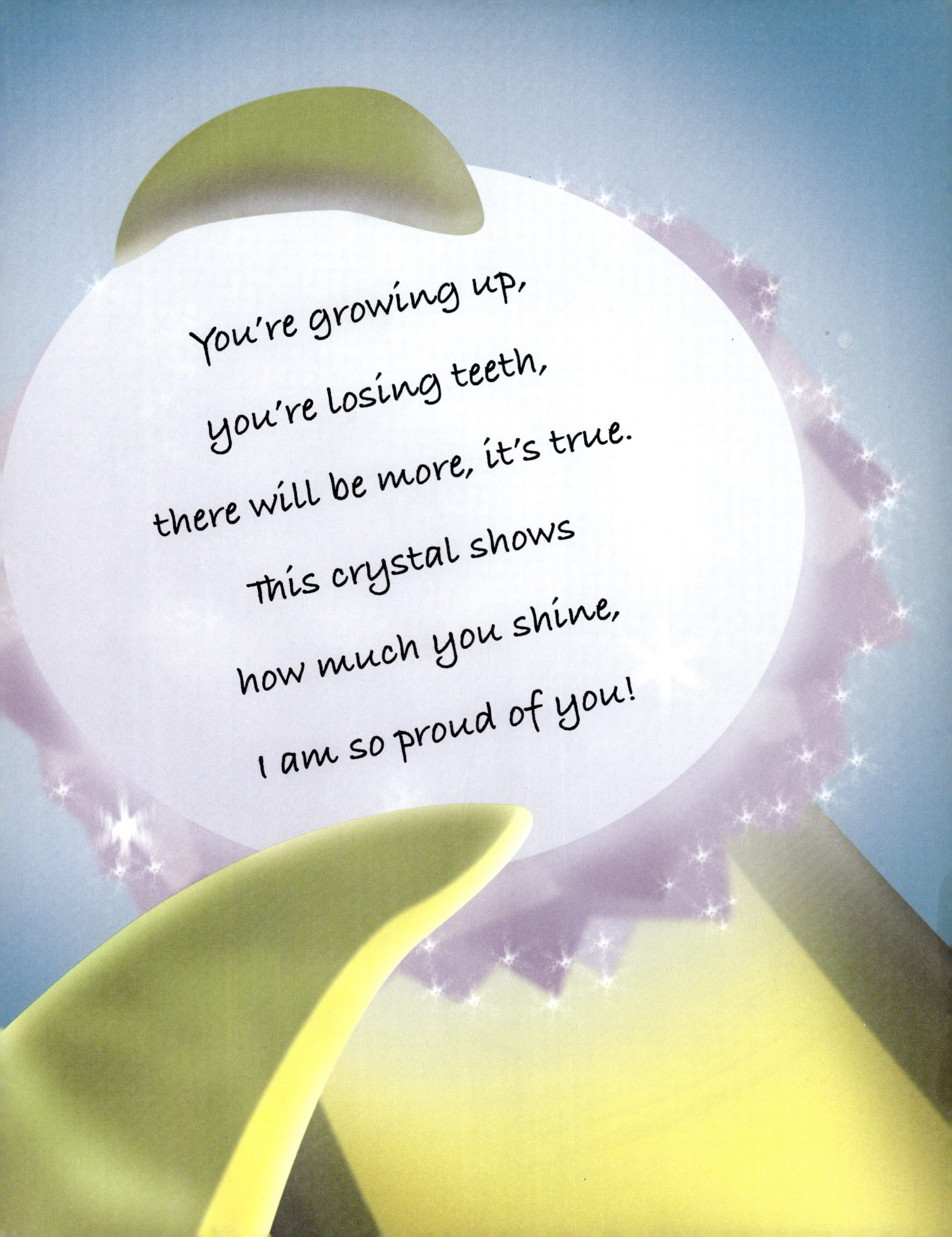

You're growing up,
you're losing teeth,
there will be more, it's true.
This crystal shows
how much you shine,
I am so proud of you!

"Do you think she'll *ever* come back?" Chomp asked.

"I don't know," his mother replied.

"It really doesn't matter," Chomp said with a big smile. "She came to the bottom of the ocean . . . just to see me!" He looked at his new crystal.

"Thank you, Tooth Fairy!"